Sports Illustrated KIDS

THE KIDS' GUIDE TO SPORTS MEDIA

BY SHANE FREDERICK

CAPSTONE PRESS
a capstone imprint

Sports Illustrated Kids is a trademark of Time Inc.
Used with permission.

Library of Congress Cataloging-in-Publication Data
Frederick, Shane.
   The kids' guide to sports media / by Shane Frederick.
      pages cm.—(Sports illustrated kids, SI kids guide books)
   Includes index.
   ISBN 978-1-4765-4152-5 (library binding)
   ISBN 978-1-4765-5184-5 (paperback)
1. Mass media and sports—Juvenile literature. 2. Communication
in sports—Juvenile literature. I. Title.
   GV742.F74 2014
   070.449796—dc23   2013032846

Editorial Credits
Anthony Wacholtz, editor; Sarah Bennett, designer; Eric Gohl,
media researcher; Charmaine Whitman, production specialist

Photo Credits
AP Photo: Stephen Chernin, 33; Corbis: David Bergman, 40; Getty
Images: MLB Photos/Josh Haunschild, 34, NBAE/Rocky Widner, 26,
Time Life Pictures/Herbert Gehr, 18, Transcendental Graphics/
Mark Rucker, 7 (bottom), WireImage/Gary Gershoff, 28, Zuffa LLC/
Christopher Capozziello, 21; Library of Congress: 8, 9; Newscom:
AP Feature Photo Service/Kurt Strumpf, 24, EPA/Erik S. Lesser,
44–45, EPA/Nic Bothma, 27, Everett Collection, 16, 19, Icon SMI/Bill
Vaughan, 43, Icon SMI/Patrick S Blood, 37, Image Broker/Siegfried
Kuttig, 39, UPI Photo Service/Terry Schmitt, 41, ZUMA Press/Keith
Birmingham, 17; Shutterstock: Annette Shaff, 32, Georgy Markov,
6, villorejo, 7 (top); Sports Illustrated: Al Tielemans, cover, 14,
Bob Martin, 5, 35 (bottom), 42, Bob Rosato, 10, David E. Klutho, 4,
36, Heinz Kluetmeier, 22, 38, John Biever, 35 (top), John Iacono, 25,
John W. McDonough, 12, 15, 20, Robert Beck, 11, 29, 31, Simon Bruty,
13, 30

Design Elements: Shutterstock

Printed in the United States of America in Stevens Point, Wisconsin.
092013   007767WZS14

TABLE OF CONTENTS

THE SPORTING LIFE

"I always turn to the sports section first.
The sports page records people's accomplishments;
the front page has nothing but man's failures."

–Earl Warren, Chief Justice of the U.S. Supreme Court (1953–1969)

The sports section Earl Warren talked about was found in his daily newspaper. But sports media go well beyond the black-and-white pages that landed on Warren's doorstep each morning. Fans follow their favorite athletes, teams, leagues, and sports in print, on the radio, on TV, and online. There's live coverage and commentary, news and networks, books and **blogs.** And, of course, there's an **app** for all of those things!

Reporters interview Patrick Kane of the Chicago Blackhawks after his team won the 2013 Stanley Cup Finals.

From box scores to Twitter, media have provided people many opportunities to follow sports over the last century. They have given fans the chance to stay up-to-date with the events that take place every day in the sports world.

blog—an online journal that is updated regularly; blog is short for web log

app—a useful program that is downloaded to computers and mobile devices; app is short for application

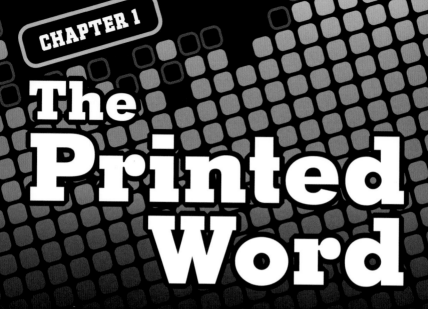

CHAPTER 1

The Printed Word

THE SPORTS PAGE

Sports, games, and athletic competitions have intrigued people for thousands of years. We know this because there are records of such events. The first Olympics and other competitions held in ancient Greece are chronicled in stories, poetry, and art. The ancient Greek poet Homer described competitions in the *Iliad*. Would that make him one of the world's first sports writers?

Homer is widely known for writing the Greek epic poems the *Iliad* and the *Odyssey*.

In more modern times, regular coverage of popular sporting activities became an important part of the newspaper. In the 1800s more and more newspapers popped up all around the United States, thanks to improvements in technology, communication, and transportation.

telegraph

Printing presses, **telegraphs,** and railroads helped spread the news, and that included news about sports.

At first boxing and horse racing dominated the sports pages. As newspapers such as the *New York World* began adding full pages and complete sections for sports, there was room for more sports. Baseball was growing in popularity, as were other team sports, such as college football and professional hockey.

It didn't take long for newspaper writers to become the authority on sports. They didn't just write stories. Their work included keeping statistics and records. A **journalist** named Henry Chadwick created the box score and, in 1858, wrote baseball's first rulebook.

Henry Chadwick (standing, right) poses with a Brooklyn baseball team in 1864.

telegraph—a system of sending messages over long distances that used wires and electrical signals

journalist—a person who gathers and reports news

The popularity of sports exploded in the United States in the years following World War I. Athletes became national heroes for their impressive performances. Writers and **columnists** contributed to the hero-making. They used colorful language and created vivid descriptions of baseball's Babe Ruth, tennis's Bill Tilden, boxing's Jack Dempsey, and Olympic swimming's Johnny Weissmuller.

New York Herald Tribune writer Grantland Rice composed a famous story in 1924 about the University of Notre Dame football team. The Irish were one of the best teams in the country at the time:

"Outlined against a blue-gray October sky, the Four Horsemen rode again. In dramatic lore they are known as Famine, Pestilence, Destruction and Death. These are only aliases. Their real names are Stuhldreher, Miller, Crowley and Layden."

Rice and other writers, such as Ring Lardner, Damon Runyon, Red Smith, and Jim Murray, achieved fame almost equal to that of the athletes they wrote about. Their way with words, as well as their ability to find unique stories, made their columns must-reads for fans following sports' biggest events.

The Four Horsemen of the 1924 Notre Dame football team

Grantland Rice

Because they cover fun and games, the sports section of a newspaper is sometimes called "the toy department." But writers have investigated the serious side of sports too. That news includes contract negotiations, crime and other off-the-field problems, performance-enhancing drug use, and the growing problem of concussions.

columnist—a person who regularly writes opinion-based articles for a newspaper, magazine, or website

WHAT'S IN YOUR PAPER?

Sports sections often focus on popular professional games and big-time college teams. But if you dig a little deeper, you'll find all kinds of stories from beyond the NFL, MLB, NBA, and NHL.

In the fall Friday nights are busy times for newsrooms throughout the United States. Those are the evenings when most high school football games are played under the lights in just about every community. Sportswriters and photographers attend some of the games and write about them for the Saturday morning paper. In the newsroom workers take calls from coaches and statisticians to include the results in print.

READ ALL ABOUT IT

In your local newspaper, there's probably coverage of girls' and boys' high school sports. If there is a university in your area, women's and men's college sports might be a focus. Some papers send reporters to local running and bicycle races. Others include the results of bowling leagues, golf tournaments, and other recreational sports. In some parts of the country, outdoor activities, such as fishing and hunting, are a staple of the sports section.

FACT

Many newspapers are members of the Associated Press and subscribe to other **wire services** to receive stories and photos from all over the world. Local editors choose which stories are most appropriate for their newspaper's audience.

wire service—a news organization that provides stories, photos, and videos to other news companies

ON THE BEAT

Many newspapers employ people to write about specific teams or sports on a daily basis. Those reporters cover teams in much the same way that police officers patrol certain neighborhoods—by walking the same route every day. Because of that rhythm and routine, the cop is said to be "on the beat." Likewise, so is the reporter.

Beat writers attend most of a particular team's games, including road games. They also go to practices, **press conferences**, and other events. For example, baseball writers might stop by a pregame batting practice, or hockey reporters can access a game-day morning skate. While there, they interview players, head coaches, assistant coaches, and other team members. They develop relationships with front-office personnel, agents, and scouts. Using all of that information, they write several stories a week.

LeBron James enjoys a press conference after the Miami Heat won the 2013 NBA Finals.

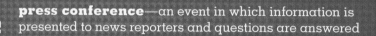

press conference—an event in which information is presented to news reporters and questions are answered

Good beat writers know the teams they cover inside and out. Readers expect them to have that knowledge so they can better understand the teams they root for. Beat writers break news about big trades, injuries, and coaching searches. They educate fans about football's wildcat offense or hockey's neutral-zone trap. They examine why a baseball player might be in a slump or why an NBA coach was fired. They analyze the NFL's salary cap or a college basketball program's recruiting success. If it has to do with their team, beat writers will be among the first to know.

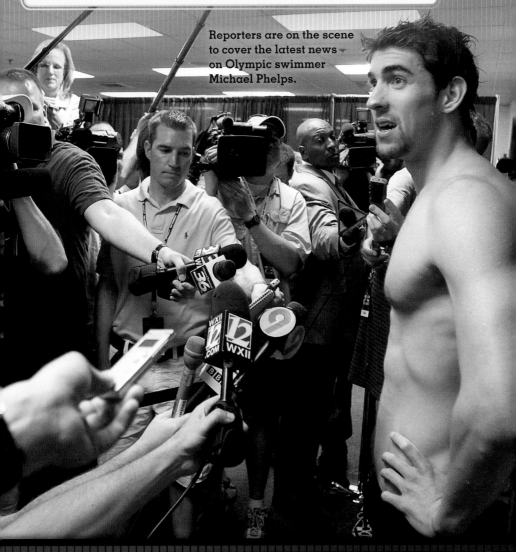

Reporters are on the scene to cover the latest news on Olympic swimmer Michael Phelps.

MAGAZINES AND BOOKS

Newspapers aren't the only places to read about the wide world of sports. Magazines give fans a chance to read in-depth personality profiles and investigative journalism pieces. They are usually longer pieces that newspapers don't always have the space for. Their bright, glossy pages are perfect for showing off eye-popping action photography.

SI photographer Robert Beck captures the action at the 2010 Winter Olympics.

When it comes to magazines, there's truly something for everyone. Some magazines cover specific sports. They give fans and players a variety of articles on their favorite pastime. Examples include *Runner's World*, *Golf*, *Tennis*, *Baseball Digest*, and *Slam*, a basketball magazine. Others, such as *Sports Illustrated* and *ESPN The Magazine*, take on the entire sports landscape.

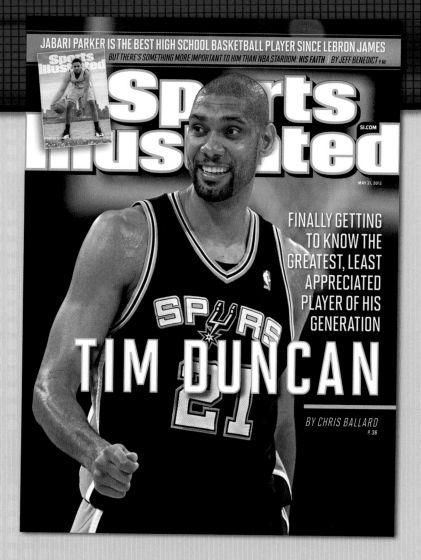

Sports Illustrated

SI.COM

MAY 21, 2012

FINALLY GETTING
TO KNOW THE
GREATEST, LEAST
APPRECIATED
PLAYER OF HIS
GENERATION

TIM DUNCAN

BY CHRIS BALLARD
P. 36

When Henry Luce began to publish *Sports Illustrated* in 1954, few people thought it would be successful. But Luce, who was the publisher of the newsmagazine *Time* and the popular *Life*, proved them wrong. Since the first issue, with Milwaukee Braves slugger Eddie Mathews on the cover, *SI* has been a staple for sports fans every week.

WANT TO DIG EVEN DEEPER INTO A SUBJECT?

There are countless books about sports. Biographies and autobiographies have been written about athletes and coaches—and even racehorses and umpires. Authors have explored the histories of sports, leagues, and teams.

CHAPTER 2

On the Air

LISTENING LIVE

The world's first commercial radio station hit the airwaves in November 1920 in Pittsburgh, Pennsylvania. It didn't take long for KDKA to discover sports would give people a reason to listen.

KDKA made history just five months after its birth. In April 1921 the station broadcast a sporting event for the first time. Listeners heard an announcer describe the blow-by-blow action of a boxing match between Johnny Ray and Johnny Dundee. That inspired a New York City-based station to air another fight, the so-called "Battle of the Century," in July. Tens of thousands of people tuned in to hear J. Andrew White's call of the heavyweight title bout between champion Jack Dempsey and Georges Carpentier.

KDKA staff in 1920, not long before their first sports broadcast

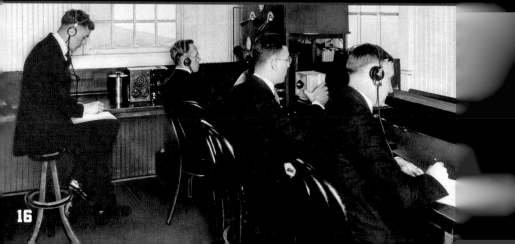

wanted in on the live action, more and more radio stations jumped on the bandwagon. Later that summer KDKA broadcast its first baseball game. It featured the hometown Pittsburgh Pirates against the Philadelphia Phillies. In the fall WJZ in New York carried the World Series between the crosstown-rival Yankees and Giants. Before the end of the decade, nationwide **networks** covered the biggest games, starting with the 1927 Rose Bowl.

Hall of Fame
broadcaster
Vin Scully

Today the radio—both over the air and by satellite—is filled with sports. Every major professional and college team has a broadcast crew and an **affiliation** with a station or a network of stations. That allows people to listen to games in their cars, homes or, really, anywhere they want. Smaller stations air high school sports for their communities. For folks in Los Angeles, Vin Scully describes the action of the Dodgers. He's been "the voice" of that baseball team for more than 60 years. He first got on the microphone in 1950 when the team still played in Brooklyn, New York.

network—a group of radio or TV stations
affiliation—the state of being closely
connected to an organization or company **17**

FEAST FOR YOUR EYES

With the success of sports on the radio, it was only natural for TV to follow. It was 1939 when games and matches started being shown right in people's living rooms. That year an NBC station broadcast the first sporting event on TV, a college baseball game between Columbia and Princeton. That same year the station carried a Major League Baseball game between the Brooklyn Dodgers and the Cincinnati Reds. It also aired a National League Football game between the Brooklyn Dodgers and the Philadelphia Eagles.

The 1939 game between Princeton and Columbia was filmed by a single camera on a wooden perch.

THE MOST POPULAR SPORT in the United States today—by far—is professional football. The main reason for that great interest is TV. In the fall millions of fans gather to watch football games on TV.

NBC aired what has since been called "The Greatest Game Ever Played" in 1958. About 45 million people tuned in on that late-December day to watch the NFL championship game between the Baltimore Colts and the New York Giants. The Colts won the thrilling game 23-17 in sudden death overtime.

Most-Watched TV Shows	
Show	**Number of Viewers**
Super Bowl XLVI, 2012 (Giants-Patriots)	111.3 million
Super Bowl XLV, 2011 (Packers-Steelers)	111.0 million
Super Bowl XLVII, 2013 (Ravens-49ers)	108.7 million
Super Bowl XLIV, 2010 (Saints-Colts)	106.5 million
M*A*S*H* series finale, 1983	106.0 million

NFL commissioner Pete Rozelle approached Roone Arledge, a broadcasting innovator for ABC, in 1969. They discussed the idea for a game to be played in **prime time**, and in 1970 Monday Night Football was born. Casting entertaining announcers such as Howard Cosell and later, John Madden, Monday Night Football became a weekly spectacle for both hard-core and casual fans. More than 40 years later, Monday nights are still highly anticipated in the NFL.

Roone Arledge

GOING PLACES

Radio and TV have given sports fans tickets to the biggest events in the world. Listeners and viewers can access the Olympics and soccer's World Cup, as well as the Super Bowl and the World Series. The Stanley Cup playoffs, the NBA Finals, college bowl games, and the NCAA Final Four come right into people's homes.

For nearly four decades, the ABC TV network aired the show *ABC's Wide World of Sports*. The weekly program often took people to various places to catch a glimpse at unique and less-popular sports. The show opened with the lines: "Spanning the globe to bring you the constant variety of sport. The thrill of victory ... and the agony of defeat ... the human drama of athletic competition." In its 1961 debut, it went to the Drake Relays track and field meet in Des Moines, Iowa. It offered bowling, auto racing, surfing, and one time, the Oklahoma Rattlesnake Hunt Championships to a mass audience. The show ran until 1998.

Sports reporter Jim Nantz (left) interviews Louisville Cardinals coach Rick Pitino as his team celebrates winning the 2013 NCAA Championship.

ESPN anchor Jorge Andres discusses an upcoming bout with mixed martial artist Miesha Tate.

A **cable television** channel called the Entertainment and Sports Programming Network made its debut in 1979 with SportsCenter, a national sports highlight show. As ESPN grew into a national, 24-hours-a-day, seven-days-a-week network, it had to fill its programming schedule. So it showed obscure sports, such as Australian rules football, the United States Football League, and America's Cup sailing.

ESPN grew into a sports media giant. It eventually obtained rights to show major college sports, as well as pro baseball, basketball, and hockey games. It landed the big fish in 1987 and aired NFL games. Today ESPN reaches more than 100 million homes.

cable television—a subscription system in which programming is sent through a series of connected cables rather than over the air

TALKING SPORTS

For many years radio broadcasts of games were mixed with non-sports programming. Music, news, and talk shows filled up much of the airtime. Announcers delivered sports scores and other news at regular times, but the sports conversation often stopped there.

In the late 1980s, a few radio stations in big cities decided to try the ESPN approach: all sports, all the time—and it worked. The first station to make the move was in New York City. The station changed its call letters to WFAN to show that it indeed was a radio station for sports fans.

Sportscaster Dan Patrick delivers a radio show from his home office.

THEY SAID IT!

Memorable calls of the game from sports' biggest moments:

"Do you believe in miracles?" —Al Michaels calling the 1980 U.S. hockey team's stunning upset of the Soviet Union in the Winter Olympics

"The Giants win the pennant!" —Russ Hodges, in 1951, calling Bobby Thomson's home run "the shot heard round the world," which gave the New York Giants the win over the Brooklyn Dodgers for the National League crown

"I don't believe what I just saw!" —Jack Buck calling Kirk Gibson's pinch-hit home run to win Game 1 of the 1988 World Series for the Los Angeles Dodgers against the Oakland Athletics

"Down goes Frazier!" —Howard Cosell calling George Foreman's first-round knockdown of unbeaten heavyweight champion Joe Frazier in 1973

Much of the programming of all-sports stations features daily hosts who talk about current events in sports. There are national shows, as well as regional and local shows. Hosts often interview special guests, such as players and coaches. But a popular part of the programming takes place when the phone lines open to the fans. The new format took sports arguments from the water coolers and playgrounds to the airwaves.

THE SERIOUS SIDE OF SPORTS

The Olympics showcase achievement in athletics every four years. TV networks pay big money for the rights to broadcast the Games and celebrate the sports.

During the 1972 Summer Olympics in Munich, West Germany, sports quickly turned to news when Palestinian terrorists took over a building in the Olympic Village. They killed an athlete, a coach, and nine other hostages from Israel. During the siege ABC Sports' **anchor** Jim McKay famously delivered updates from the horrifying scene. He stayed on the air for 16 hours as the news unfolded.

In an iconic image of the 1972 Olympics, one of the terrorists appeared on the balcony of the building where the hostages were being held.

McKay showed that his media skills went well beyond the sidelines. When serious news happens at sporting events, the TV reporters, newspaper writers, and radio broadcasters work to provide the latest information to their audiences.

anchor—a person who presents and coordinates a live TV news program

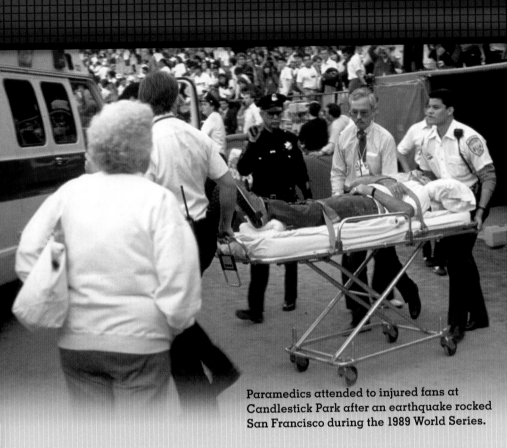

Paramedics attended to injured fans at Candlestick Park after an earthquake rocked San Francisco during the 1989 World Series.

Al Michaels was nominated for a news Emmy for his coverage of the major earthquake that shook the cities of San Francisco and Oakland during the 1989 World Series. The quake began just before the San Francisco Giants and Oakland Athletics were about to start Game 3. Michaels remained on the air, even after the game was postponed, to report on the tragedy that killed about 60 people and injured thousands more.

FACT

In 2013 sports reporters from multiple outlets, including *Runner's World* magazine, gave reports of the bombs that exploded at the finish line of the Boston Marathon.

CHAPTER 3

The Tangled Web

RIGHT AT YOUR FINGERTIPS

Technology continues to change the landscape of sports media. Print was the first medium to reach a large number of people. The audiences grew with radio and television, sending live sports into cars and homes. But nothing shook things up like the Internet. The web and wireless technology combined all of the existing media and dropped them onto people's laps via laptop computers. It also put them into their hands with tablets and smartphones.

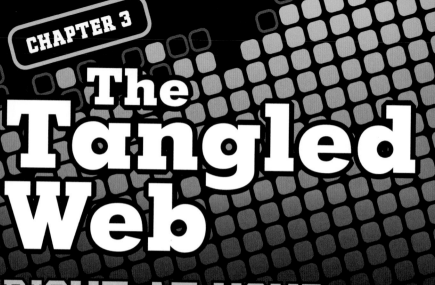

NBA star Stephen Curry uses his computer while stretching before a game.

information from games. Fans can check fantasy football statistics in real time. They can check the injury status of a favorite player or follow the commentary of writers live from press row. They can view highlights of monster dunks and circus catches or simply sit back and watch the games on their devices.

A fan takes pictures with his iPad at a 2013 soccer match in Africa.

ESPN and Yahoo are the big guns in the online sports industry. Their sites feature numerous bloggers and other contributors. Several newspaper writers and columnists even jumped to the new medium. You name it, it's covered—pro leagues, college conferences, and fantasy sports. The sites regularly compete with the so-called traditional media for breaking news and information.

Most-Visited Sports Websites	
Website	Monthly Visitors
1. Yahoo! Sports	125.2 million
2. ESPN	75.5 million
3. BleacherReport	38 million
4. CBSSports	28 million
5. Sports Illustrated	20 million

Source: http://www.ebizmba.com/ articles/sports-websites (November 2013)

There was a time when the word "blogger" made people think of super fans typing comments from their couches. But blogs and sites not tied to the traditional media quickly became serious parts of the business of covering sports.

Will Leitch began a site called Deadspin in 2005. It took an **irreverent** look at sports, sometimes exposing athletes' off-the-field antics— both good and bad. It used humor to poke fun at famous sports figures. It became wildly popular and even began to later break stories picked up by traditional media outlets.

Will Leitch

Now owned by Yahoo, the Rivals website explores the competitive world of college football and basketball recruiting. Its site tracks and ranks high school athletes and breaks news about what universities the top recruits pick. Rivals also gives fans of high schools and colleges a forum—a message board—to communicate with each other.

Bill Simmons was known as the Boston Sports Guy when he penned a regular column for his own website. But that turned into a job as a national sports guy for ESPN.com in 1997. Following in the footsteps of the hero-makers of the 1920s, Simmons became famous. He wrote a book about the NBA, appeared on TV, and started his own **podcast**. He eventually launched Grantland.com, a magazine-style site that covers sports and pop culture. The site was named after sports media pioneer Grantland Rice.

Bill Simmons works on a sports story from home.

irreverent—treating something in a way that is not serious or respectful

podcast—an online audio or video show available to be downloaded to a computer or other device

ONLINE NEWSPAPERS

Today's beat reporters no longer just file a story or two for the next day's newspaper. They arrive at the parks and stadiums early and stay late. They put all of the information they gather online as soon— and as often—as possible. They update blogs and write exclusive stories for the paper's website.

After the game—and sometimes during—they might do a live blog or "chat" with fans. They answer questions and discuss the action or the progress of the team. They might shoot video of an interview or press conference with a smartphone to post to a blog or an online channel. They could also record a conversation for a podcast. Somewhere along the line, they will indeed write that story for the print edition. But the story is often available to read on a website hours before the actual paper is delivered.

Sportswriters attend games to cover the action as it happens.

For newspapers, the web has given a medium with limited space an unlimited amount of room to provide more and more information for its readers. And when it comes to sports, those readers constantly crave more knowledge about their favorite teams.

THE TWITTER GENERATION

Many people in the sports world quickly embraced social media as useful tools to put out information. That was especially true with Twitter shortly after it appeared in 2006. While each post—or "tweet"—consists of only 140 **characters**, journalists find it to be a useful tool in their coverage of teams and events. Their audience is made up of followers—Twitter users who subscribe to a particular feed. Fans of the New York Yankees, for instance, might follow beat writers from the many newspapers that cover the team. They can also follow bloggers, broadcasters, and even members of the team.

http://twitter.com/

twitter

Follow your interests
Instant updates from your friends, industry experts, favor celebrities, and what's happening around the world.

Search Twitter

character—an individual symbol such as a letter or a number

FUTURE FAN EXPERIENCE

The Game · Video Booth · Team Stats · Concessions

yankees.com

Reporters use Twitter to send up-to-the-second updates from games, practices, and press conferences. They use it to post links to their own online stories, columns, photographs, and videos. They also use it to put out facts and opinions about the teams they cover, as well as links to information fans might find interesting. Broadcasters use it to make their coverage more interactive with viewers and listeners. Teams use Twitter as another way to get news out. A football team might tweet its training camp schedule, while a baseball team might use it to warn fans of a rainout or a delay.

Media outlets also use Facebook to post links to stories and promote the work they are doing. Teams use social media to promote themselves too. They upload photos and highlight videos. They also encourage interaction among their fans.

SPEAKING THEIR MIND

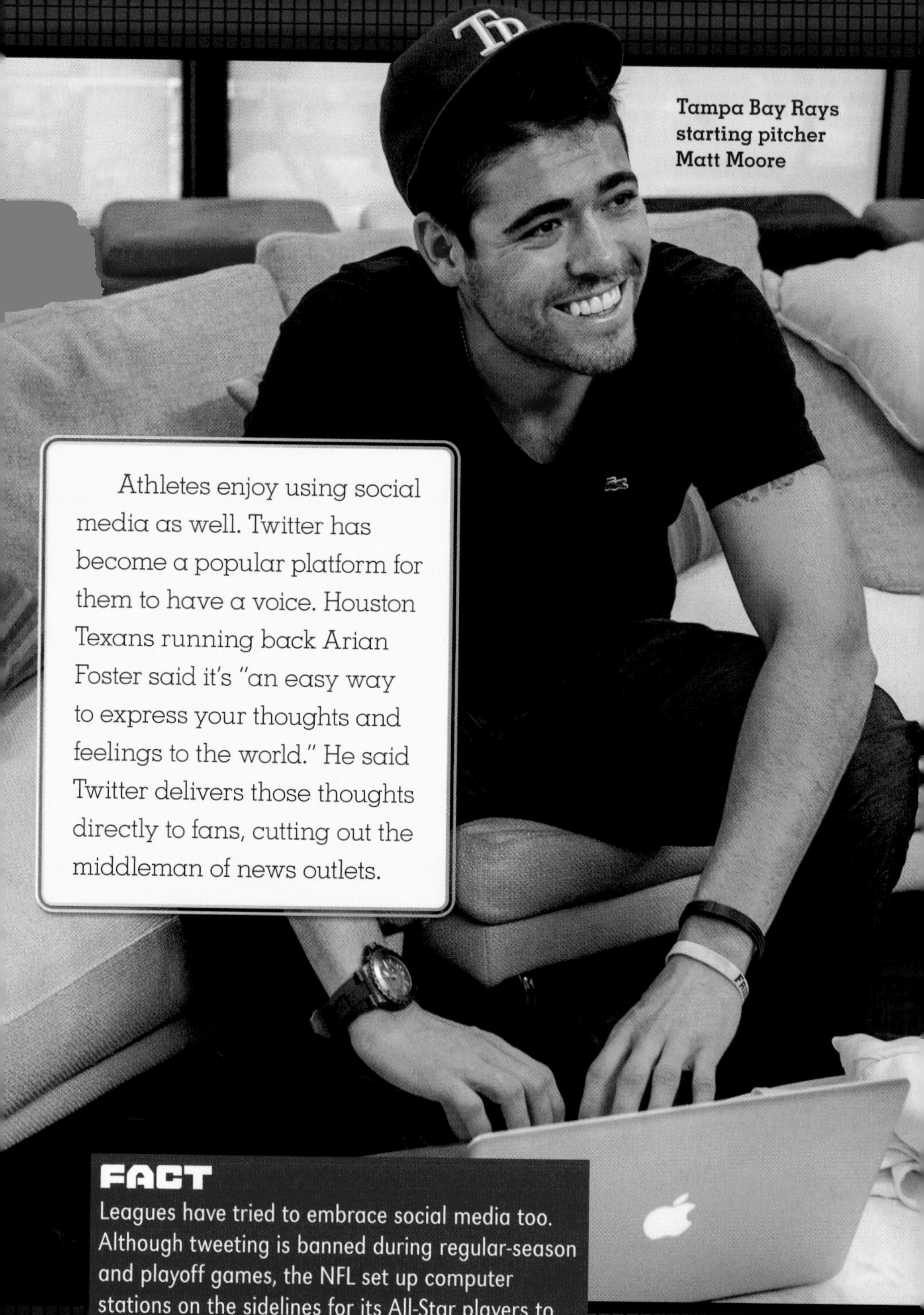

Tampa Bay Rays
starting pitcher
Matt Moore

Athletes enjoy using social media as well. Twitter has become a popular platform for them to have a voice. Houston Texans running back Arian Foster said it's "an easy way to express your thoughts and feelings to the world." He said Twitter delivers those thoughts directly to fans, cutting out the middleman of news outlets.

FACT
Leagues have tried to embrace social media too. Although tweeting is banned during regular-season and playoff games, the NFL set up computer stations on the sidelines for its All-Star players to tweet during the Pro Bowl.

Athletes quickly found out, however, that they have to be careful with their tweets. During Twitter's early days, Milwaukee Bucks forward Charlie Villanueva got in a little trouble for tweeting during halftime of a 2009 game. Coach Scott Skiles said he didn't want his players to give the impression that they weren't focused on the basketball game.

Others have been fined or suspended for tweeting inappropriate comments. The NBA fined Dallas Mavericks owner Mark Cuban $50,000 for complaining about the league's referees on Twitter. Some college coaches have decided to avoid the hassle and have banned their athletes from using Twitter.

Mark Cuban

Cristiano Ronaldo

Most-Followed Sports Figures on Twitter

The most-followed sports figure is soccer player Cristiano Ronaldo of Real Madrid (Spain) with 22.8 million followers. The top female athlete is tennis player Serena Williams with 4 million followers. The most-followed players by league are:

Player	Number of Followers
NBA: LeBron James	10.5 million
NFL: Chad Johnson	3.7 million
PGA: Tiger Woods	3.7 million
MLB: Nick Swisher	1.7 million
NHL: Alex Ovechkin	627,000

Source: http://www.tweeting-athletes.com/TopAthletes.cfm (November 2013)

CONNECTING
TO THE FANS

For many years sports teams relied on the media to send messages to mass audiences. Sports information directors and media relations managers sent **press releases** and pitched story ideas. The hope was that reporters might find those stories interesting and deliver that information—or even a small part of it—to their audiences.

St. Louis Blues forward David Backes talks to the media after a 2012 victory over the Anaheim Ducks.

REPORTING ON THEMSELVES

The Los Angeles Kings made headlines in 2009 when it hired a beat reporter away from the *Los Angeles Daily News*. The Kings assigned Rich Hammond to cover the team for the Kings' website. Hammond was allowed to cover the team as he did for the newspaper, and the team said it would not **censor** his stories and columns. Other teams have followed suit, while league sites such as MLB.com have hired reporters to cover each baseball team.

Fans can use mobile devices to record the action at the ballpark.

Teams still maintain close relationships with the reporters who cover them and continue to inform them about the latest happenings. But they no longer have to solely rely on outsiders to spread their news. With their own websites and social media, teams, leagues, and college athletic programs put out all sorts of information for fans. Their sites include breaking news, feature stories, highlights, interviews, and statistics. Some even broadcast live video of events, including games, announcements, and press conferences.

press release—an official statement from an organization sent to news organizations

censor—to remove material an organization considers objectionable

CHAPTER 4

Working in Sports Media

WORKING IN PRINT

To get a job as a sports writer for a newspaper or magazine, you need to have a passion for and a knowledge of sports. Watch, learn, and read about sports of all kinds, not just the ones you play or follow. Stay up to date on the latest sports news and trends.

Alex Montag, a kid reporter for *Sports Illustrated Kids*, visited the New York Mets clubhouse at Citi Field.

You'll probably need a college degree. Journalism or English are two majors that will help prepare you for a media career. Write or edit for the college newspaper or another publication. That way you can gain experience asking questions and reporting. Since most colleges have sports teams, cover a team for the paper. Build up your experience and collect your **clips**.

Since most newspapers have a website and use social media, experience using multimedia tools is a must. Learn to take photographs, shoot and edit video, and record audio. You could even start your own blog.

Working for a newspaper can be an exciting, rewarding career. It's more than seeing the exciting action of a big game firsthand. You also are the one others trust to give them the inside scoop about what happened in the game.

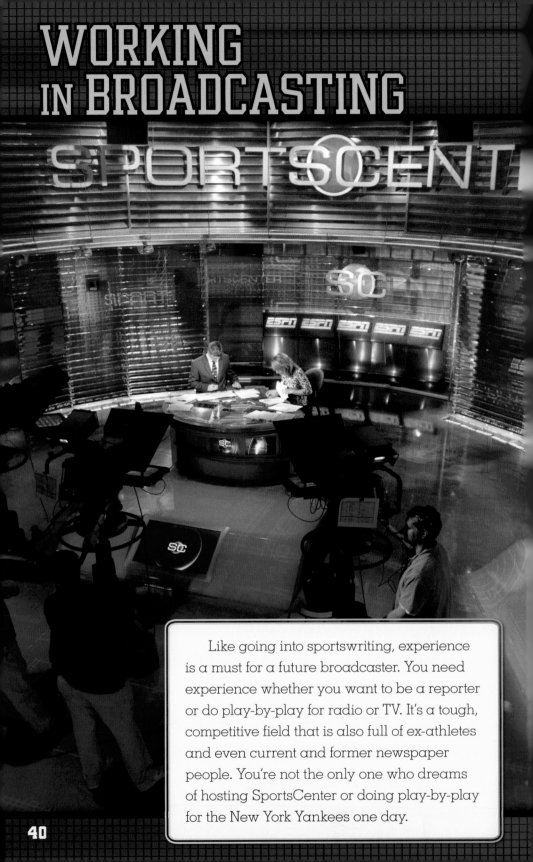

WORKING
IN BROADCASTING

Like going into sportswriting, experience is a must for a future broadcaster. You need experience whether you want to be a reporter or do play-by-play for radio or TV. It's a tough, competitive field that is also full of ex-athletes and even current and former newspaper people. You're not the only one who dreams of hosting SportsCenter or doing play-by-play for the New York Yankees one day.

A college degree is a must. Major in broadcasting, communications, or journalism. Some colleges have state-of-the-art studios and field equipment that give students hands-on experience. They learn what it's like in front of and behind the camera. Apply for an internship at a radio station, TV station, or network. Bring a **reel** to show to potential employers.

Hone your skills as a public speaker, but also be the best writer you can be. With all of that experience and maybe a little luck, you'll be reading those words to millions of people one day.

WOMEN'S WORK

Lesley Visser became the first female NFL beat writer in 1976 working for the *Boston Globe*. Her press pass actually said women weren't allowed in the press box. But she did her job well, just like so many other women in sports media. It has been a struggle, though. Time Inc. sued Major League Baseball after its *Sports Illustrated* writer, Melissa Ludtke, was denied the same locker room access given to male reporters during the 1977 World Series. Time Inc. and Ludtke won the suit, which paved the way for many more women to go into sports journalism.

Lesley Visser

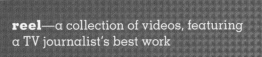

reel—a collection of videos, featuring a TV journalist's best work

BEHIND THE SCENES

It's easy to take for granted how sports reach you through the media, whether it's in print, over the airwaves, or online. There are many people involved in each part of the process.

Newspapers and magazines employ sports editors who assign stories and plan coverage. Copy editors correct grammatical errors and other mistakes. Photographers bring their own brand of journalism, capturing moments in time to help tell the stories. Designers help bring the pages to life as they combine the words and pictures.

Radio broadcasts employ producers who plan and organize the shows. They find topics to discuss, line up guests to interview, and choose which callers will be heard. Radio stations also have engineers who keep everything on the air.

Television broadcasts, especially of games, require dozens of people to make sure everything goes smoothly. The director calls the shots, as camera operators, audio and video engineers, graphics operators, and production assistants do their jobs. It happens at a frantic pace inside the production truck, but it all comes together on your TV screen.

FACT

The first televised NFL game had two cameras recording the action. In Super Bowl XLVII in 2013, CBS had 62 cameras stationed in various locations around the Superdome.

WORKING
FOR THE TEAM

Professional teams and college athletic departments employ people to deliver their messages to the media and to fans. There are many titles for those positions, including media relations, public relations, communications personnel, and college sports information directors. People who work in those departments have many tasks. Most importantly, they serve as spokespeople and media **liaisons**. They are often the direct connection between the teams and the reporters who cover them.

San Francisco 49ers players take questions from reporters the day before Super Bowl XLVII.

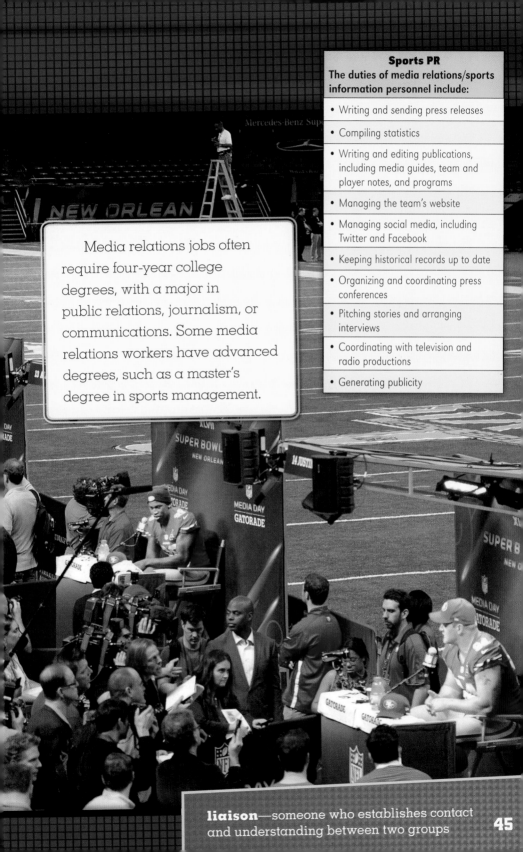

Media relations jobs often require four-year college degrees, with a major in public relations, journalism, or communications. Some media relations workers have advanced degrees, such as a master's degree in sports management.

liaison—someone who establishes contact and understanding between two groups

GLOSSARY

affiliation—the state of being closely connected to an organization or company

anchor—a person who presents and coordinates a live TV news program

app—a useful program that is downloaded to computers and mobile devices; app is short for application

blog—an online journal that is updated regularly; blog is short for web log

cable television—a subscription system in which programming is sent through a series of connected cables rather than over the air

censor—to remove material an organization considers objectionable

character—an individual symbol such as a letter or a number

clip—an individual story cut out of a newspaper or magazine, often part of a writer's best work

columnist—a person who regularly writes opinion-based articles for a newspaper, magazine, or website

irreverent—treating something in a way that is not serious or respectful

journalist—a person who gathers and reports news

liaison—someone who establishes contact and understanding between two groups

network—a group of radio or television stations

podcast—an online audio or video show available to be downloaded to a computer or other device

press conference—an event in which information is presented to news reporters and questions are answered

press release—an official statement from an organization sent out to news organizations

prime time—a block of TV programming in the middle of the evening

reel—a collection of videos, featuring a TV journalist's best work

telegraph—a system of sending messages over long distances that used wires and electrical signals

wire service—a news organization that provides stories, photos, and videos to other news companies

READ MORE

Editors of **Sports Illustrated Kids** magazine.
*Sports Illustrated Kids: The Big Book of Why Sports
Edition.* New York: Time Home Entertainment, Inc., 2012.

Frederick, Shane. *The Technology of Football.*
Sports Illustrated Kids. North Mankato, Minn.:
Capstone Press, 2013.

Teitelbaum, Michael. *Sports Broadcasting.*
Ann Arbor, Mich.: Cherry Lake Pub., 2009.

Witmer, Scott. *Sports and Society.*
Chicago: Heinemann Library, 2012.

INTERNET SITES

FactHound offers a safe, fun way to find Internet sites
related to this book. All of the sites on FactHound
have been researched by our staff.

Here's all you do:

Visit *www.facthound.com*

Type in this code: 9781476541525

Super-cool stuff!

Check out projects, games and lots more at
www.capstonekids.com

INDEX